MIWOK

Big Buddy Books
An Imprint of Abdo Publishing
abdopublishing.com

Katie Lajiness

abdopublishing.com

Published by Abdo Publishing, a division of ABDO, PO Box 398166, Minneapolis, Minnesota 55439.
Copyright © 2017 by Abdo Consulting Group, Inc. International copyrights reserved in all countries. No part
of this book may be reproduced in any form without written permission from the publisher. Big Buddy Books™
is a trademark and logo of Abdo Publishing.

Printed in the United States of America, North Mankato, Minnesota.
062016
092016

Cover Photo: ASSOCIATED PRESS; Shutterstock.com.
Interior Photos: ASSOCIATED PRESS (p. 5); © Nancy Carter/North Wind Picture Archives (p. 9); © iStockphoto.com
    (pp. 21, 27); © Charles Mann/Alamy (p. 19); Lawrence Migdale/Photo Researchers, Inc. (p. 29); © NativeStock.com/
    AngelWynn (pp. 10, 11, 13, 15, 16, 17); © Michael Nicholson/Corbis (p. 26); © North Wind Picture Archives (p. 23);
    © david sanger photography/Alamy (p. 15); Shutterstock.com (p. 25); © ZUMA Press, Inc./Alamy (p. 30).

Quote on page 30 from the Yosemite Conservancy.

Coordinating Series Editor: Tamara L. Britton
Graphic Design: Adam Craven

Library of Congress Cataloging-in-Publication Data

Lajiness, Katie, author.
  Miwok / Katie Lajiness.
Minneapolis, MN : ABDO Publishing Company, 2017. | Series:
  Native Americans
LCCN 2015050492| ISBN 9781680782004 | ISBN 9781680774955 (ebook)
Miwok Indians--History--Juvenile literature. | Miwok
  Indians--Social life and customs--Juvenile literature.
LCC E99.M69 L28 2017 | DDC 970.004/974133--dc23
LC record available at http://lccn.loc.gov/2015050492

CONTENTS

Amazing People

Hundreds of years ago, North America was mostly wild, open land. Native American tribes lived on the land. They had their own languages and **customs**.

The Miwok (MEE-wahk) are one Native American tribe. They are known for basket weaving and stone hunting tools. Let's learn more about these Native Americans.

Did You Know?

The name *Miwok* means "people."

Miwok dancers often paint their faces and wear feathers in their hair.

MIWOK TERRITORY

Miwok homelands were in what is now central California. There were four Miwok tribes. The Sierra Miwok made up the largest group. They lived at the base of the Sierra Nevada.

The Coast Miwok lived near what is now San Francisco, California. The Lake Miwok were farther north. The Bay and Plains Miwok settled along the San Joaquin and Sacramento rivers.

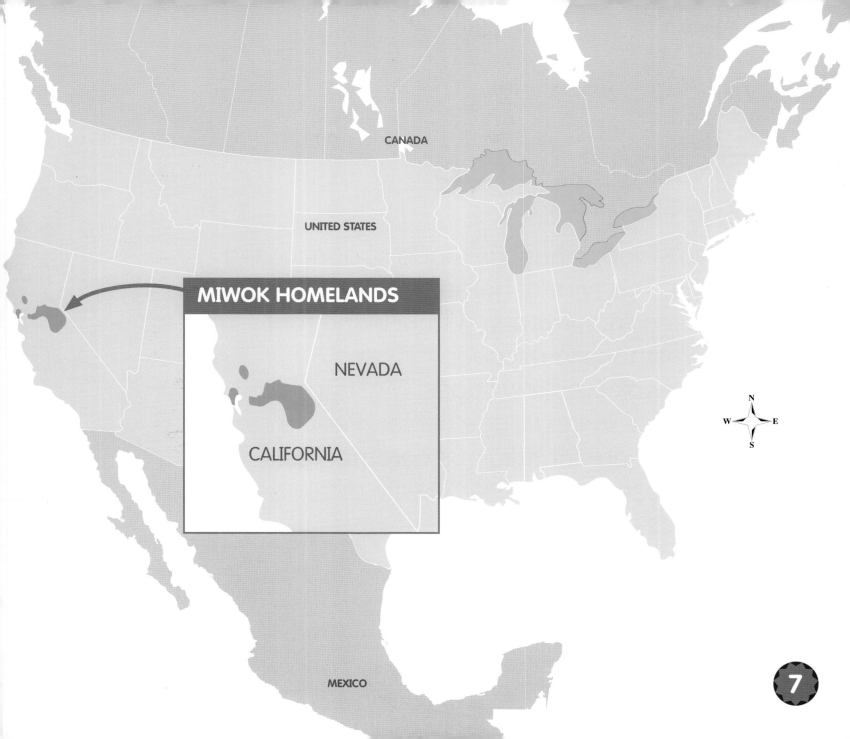

CANADA

UNITED STATES

MIWOK HOMELANDS

NEVADA

CALIFORNIA

MEXICO

N
W E
S

HOME LIFE

Miwok lived in houses made of bark called lean-tos. This type of home was easy to build and lasted many years. A hole in the roof allowed smoke to escape.

The Miwok lived in villages. Most had a roundhouse in the village center. People gathered there for religious **ceremonies**. Roundhouses were covered with dirt and grass.

Lean-tos were built with wooden frames. Bark kept the outside of the home dry.

9

What They Ate

The Miwok were skilled fishermen, hunters, and gatherers. Men fished for sturgeon and salmon. And, they used bows and arrows to hunt birds and deer.

Women gathered nuts, berries, and roots. Acorns were a common food. The Miwok had special buildings to store acorns. The stored acorns could be ground into flour to make mush or soup.

Fish were part of the Miwok's meals. Men often used sharp tools to catch fish.

Miwok ate blackberries, deer meat, and acorn soup for many meals.

DAILY LIFE

Most Miwok communities had a sweathouse. Men used sweathouses before hunting to remove their human scent.

The Miwok's clothes were simple. In cold weather, people wore deerskin moccasins. Men wore **loincloths**. Sometimes, they wore animal-skin capes. Women made grass skirts and dresses. Usually, young children did not wear clothes.

Miwok sweathouses were dug into the ground.

In a Miwok village, people had different jobs. Men fished and hunted. Women cared for the children. They also made clothes and baskets. They decorated them with beads and feathers.

Miwok women used tule reeds to weave baskets. These baskets were used to gather food for the village.

Miwok baskets featured woven patterns with geometric shapes, plants, and animals.

MADE BY HAND

The Miwok made many objects by hand. They often used natural materials. These arts and crafts added beauty to everyday life.

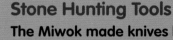

Stone Hunting Tools
The Miwok made knives by shaping stones until they had sharp edges.

Cocoon Rattles

Miwok combined moth cocoons, a wooden handle, beads, and animal fur to make a rattle. This was used as an instrument during ceremonies.

Woven Skirts

Miwok women made skirts out of grass, seeds, and leather.

Shell Fishhooks

The Miwok living along the California coast made fishhooks out of seashells.

Spirit Life

Mount Diablo was a special place for the Miwok people. They believed the earth was formed from the top of the mount. Miwok believed an animal god called Coyote created the Native American people at Mount Diablo.

Like many tribes, the Miwok had **ceremonies** and **rituals**. A **shaman** was in charge of ceremonies. The Miwok believed he could heal the sick. They thought old dancers could cure the sick through music and dancing.

The Miwok performed many different dances.
Some dances required special clothing.

STORYTELLERS

Stories are important to the Miwok. Some stories teach people about the tribe's way of life. Others are shared for fun.

Coyotes are common characters in many Miwok stories. There are also stories about magical birds.

The Miwok had great respect for coyotes. They believed coyotes were blessed animals. So, they did not hunt them.

Fighting for Land

Long ago, many Miwok villages lived in peace. Over time, outsiders arrived and took their land. In the 1820s and 1830s, the Miwok fought the Spanish to maintain their territory.

In 1848, US settlers traveled to California to look for gold. They hurt many Miwok and took tribal land. Then the US Army arrived. The soldiers killed many Miwok when the tribes refused to give up their land.

Thousands of men traveled to California in search of gold and fortune. They forced the Miwok off the land. Then settlers built towns near the gold sites.

23

From 1900 to 1920, the US government set up small Miwok settlements. However, most of these ended beginning in the 1930s.

Without land, many Miwok gave up their **traditions**. They moved away and found work on farms. In the 1970s, some Miwok tribes returned to their traditional homelands.

The Transcontinental Railroad was completed in 1869. It cut through Miwok lands, bringing even more settlers.

BACK IN TIME

1579

The Miwok met British explorer Francis Drake.

1769

The Spanish began to build **missions** in California. Many Miwok became **Catholics**.

1811

The Spanish made many Miwok move to the San Jose **Mission**. There, the Miwok were forced to work for the Spanish.

1848

California became a US territory. Gold was discovered in the Sierra Nevada. Many settlers moved into the area and took over the Miwok's land.

1910

European sicknesses and fighting with settlers brought the Miwok population down to about 700.

1972–1994

Several Miwok groups regained tribal recognition from the US government. They began to run small settlements again.

THE MIWOK TODAY

The Miwok have a long, rich history. They are remembered for their stories and tribal **rituals**.

Miwok roots run deep. Today, the people have kept alive those special things that make them Miwok. Even though times have changed, many people carry the **traditions**, stories, and memories of the past into the present.

Did You Know?

In 2010, there were about 3,500 Miwok living in the United States.

Young Miwok still dance at festivals and tribal events.

"… I'm sitting among the masters' work. Every day they're telling me, 'Don't forget our ways, Julia. Keep talking, keep telling people about it.' I've worked with all kinds of women, and they all tell me to teach, to tell everybody about my baskets and how I make them."

– Julia Parker, Miwok
　　Cultural Demonstrator

Glossary

Catholic a member of the Roman Catholic Church. This kind of Christianity has been around since the first century and is led by the pope.

ceremony a formal event on a special occasion.

custom a practice that has been around a long time and is common to a group or a place.

loincloth a simple cloth worn by a man to cover his lower body.

mission a place where religious work is done.

ritual (RIH-chuh-wuhl) a formal act or set of acts that is repeated.

shaman a person who is believed to be able to use magic to heal sickness or see the future.

tradition (truh-DIH-shuhn) a belief, a custom, or a story handed down from older people to younger people.

Websites

To learn more about Native Americans, visit **booklinks.abdopublishing.com**. These links are routinely monitored and updated to provide the most current information available.

INDEX